SEO for WordPress Blogs
Rank #1 on Google in any Niche or Keywords Guaranteed

Search Engine Optimization White Hat Practice to Rank High on Google and Other Major Search Engines (Boost your SERP)

Smit Chacha

This book is a guide to how to rank #1 on Google and other search engines. I have been writing WordPress blogs for over 10 years and my blogs are ranked very high on major search engines. I solely use pure 100% White Hat SEO techniques to rank high on search engine results or SERP.

Getting a ton of web organic traffic is what this book is all about. You will learn the power of social media marketing and email marketing and how to rank high in Google and other search engines.

Pure White Hat SEO methods to rank on Google and other search engines.

The techniques and tips shared in this book will also help your current WordPress blogs if they have been penalized by Google from their Google algorithm updates (Panda, Penguin, Hummingbird or any other update).

The guideline in this book is proven to give quality results and you should be ranked #1 within 3 to 6 months' time, after implementing all the tips, tactics and techniques found in this bestselling guide book.

Learn all the best onsite and offsite White Hat SEO techniques and work in ranking high on Google and other major search engines.

Find out the best WordPress plugins to do SEO that works. Learn which WordPress Themes work better in ranking on the search engine results or SERP.

And find out how to stand as a brand online. As a bonus

SEO for WordPress Blogs
Rank #1 on Google in any Niche or Keywords Guaranteed
Search Engine Optimization White Hat Practice to Rank High on Google and Other
Major Search Engines (Boost your SERP)

you will also get tips in how to make money with your
WordPress blog and content.

SEO Introduction

Before I jump straight to the book let me first tell you a little bit about me. My name is Smit Chacha and I have been successfully doing WordPress SEO for the past 10 years! I was able to rank #1 on Google and other search engines in several niches and keywords. Even after Panda, Penguin and Hummingbird Google updates.

You can search my name on Google and you will find a ton of details about myself. I have successfully done online marketing for the past 10 years. I have developed countless WordPress blogs and websites and done affiliate marketing, social media marketing, video marketing, SEO, content marketing and e-commerce.

I have made thousands of dollars online with simple SEO and marketing tricks that I want to share with you in this book. The formula to rank #1 on Google and other search engines in simple and easy to implement and

SEO for WordPress Blogs
Rank #1 on Google in any Niche or Keywords Guaranteed
Search Engine Optimization White Hat Practice to Rank High on Google and Other
Major Search Engines (Boost your SERP)

anyone can do it.

Every single tip and trick shared in this book is done within Google guidelines and therefore there are safe to do and implements. Pure 100% white hat SEO techniques that will lift your blog on the search engines in no time.

Before Google updates many webmasters used black hat techniques to rank higher on search engines and they used to work. Ranking on the web was very easy. After a while Google and other search engines reviewed their algorithm and done few updates on the life, which caused many webmasters to collapse or even bankrupt their web rankings.

Google updates caused a huge chaos and many webmasters got punished and their WordPress blogs drop rankings or even worse cases where blogs where simple de-indexed by Google.

These blogs where after a few years re-indexed and ranked on search engines after webmasters reviewing their SEO tactics and doing lots of tweaks on their websites.

This means that if you follow the Google guidelines you can always rank #1 in the major search engines. I am not

SEO for WordPress Blogs
Rank #1 on Google in any Niche or Keywords Guaranteed
Search Engine Optimization White Hat Practice to Rank High on Google and Other
Major Search Engines (Boost your SERP)

encouraging anyone to start with Blackhat SEO. These tactics worked in the past and since than Google has become a lot smarter and it will de-index your website instantly, specially if it is a newly build blog.

Grey Hat SEO is another term and this term simply means getting back from Black Hat SEO to White Hat SEO. And as discussed earlier this technique does not work anymore! Avoid Black Hat and Grey Hat, just focus on pure White Hat SEO techniques. Follow the guidelines and you will be ranked #1 in all major search engines out there.

What Google and other major search engines is trying to say to webmasters is that the web has matured, however it is still in their infancy, past methods and tricks are no longer tolerated. The tolerance level of Google and other major search engines towards Black Hat and Grey Hat has become a lot shorter than before. Nowadays Google and other major search engines are a lot smarter in tackling Black Hat and Grey Hat SEO techniques and they will de-index your blog very quickly.

So just avoid those no longer tolerated tactics and focus on pure White Hat SEO and you will rule the web in any niche or keyword.

White Hat SEO takes time for a newly built website or

SEO for WordPress Blogs
Rank #1 on Google in any Niche or Keywords Guaranteed
Search Engine Optimization White Hat Practice to Rank High on Google and Other
Major Search Engines (Boost your SERP)

blog can take up to 6 months to start seeing the results. But they are guaranteed to work. Now let's jump to SEO for WordPress Blogs.

Installing WordPress Blogs on your Webhost

WordPress in widely used and most favourite platform loved by Google and other major search engines. It is very easy to use and install. For any website or blog you will need a web host and most web host offer a quick install setup in the CPanel.

Simply use that source to install WordPress. Hostgator is my favourite web host, I have been using it for many years and they offer extremely high rated customer service. They also offer quick install setup for WordPress on the CPanel.

SEO for WordPress Blogs
Rank #1 on Google in any Niche or Keywords Guaranteed
Search Engine Optimization White Hat Practice to Rank High on Google and Other
Major Search Engines (Boost your SERP)

Figure 1 - https://www.hostgator.com/

If you are having difficulties in installing WordPress just ask the web host team and follow the guidelines. This book is not about how to use WordPress from scratch it is about SEO for WordPress. And I am assuming that you already have knowledge of WordPress and possessed a WordPress blog.

SEO for WordPress Blogs
Rank #1 on Google in any Niche or Keywords Guaranteed
Search Engine Optimization White Hat Practice to Rank High on Google and Other
Major Search Engines (Boost your SERP)

SEO Yoast for WordPress

Figure 2 - https://yoast.com/wordpress/plugins/seo/

This is my favourite SEO plugin for WordPress. There is a
free version and a premium. The free version in

SEO for WordPress Blogs
Rank #1 on Google in any Niche or Keywords Guaranteed
Search Engine Optimization White Hat Practice to Rank High on Google and Other
Major Search Engines (Boost your SERP)

sufficient for doing pure 100% White Hat SEO. I use it on all my blogs and websites. It is easy to use and install.

The reason why you want the Yoast SEO plugin is because it has some special features that plain WordPress does not have. These special features allow you to do extreme powerful onsite SEO.

Onsite SEO

As you may know there are 2 types of SEO. Onsite SEO and offsite SEO, there difference is that onsite SEO means the SEO of your inner pages on the website or blog. This type to SEO is easily implemented and you have lots of control. The offsite SEO means the SEO that is not controlled by you (somewhat). Offsite SEO means getting backlinks from other sources of the web. Basically, you can a backlink pointing to your website that is placed on someone else website or blog. The authority of these backlinks will matter in how Google and other search engines sees your blog as a White Hat or Back Hat.

For onsite SEO the SEO Yoast plugin is very powerful. Install that plugin and start using it. What you want is to add breadcrumbs on your pages and focus on a page

SEO for WordPress Blogs
Rank #1 on Google in any Niche or Keywords Guaranteed
Search Engine Optimization White Hat Practice to Rank High on Google and Other
Major Search Engines (Boost your SERP)

title that is under 54 characters with at least 2 of your keywords that you want to rank. The page description must be under 128 characters with at least 3 to 4 keywords in it that you want to rank. However, this section, page description, must be filled manually and it must be humanly readable.

The key to rank #1 on Google and other major search engines is to have high quality content that is humanly readable without the computerised keyword rich text. If you use keyword rich text it will catch Google eyes and label you as a Black Hat SEO webmaster.

Your blogpost should be at least 500 to 800 words long with images and alt text. The keywords must be highlighted with H2, H3 and H4 tags. Plus, the paragraphs of your blogposts should be humanly readable with maximum of 2 keywords per 150 words. If you follow this guideline you will rank #1 on Google and other search engines in terms of onsite SEO.

Note: *whenever it is possible to inner link your blogpost, do it with an inner link in your posts. These inner links will get link juice if they get ranked quicker. This technique is widely used by Wikipedia. And any inner link should be highlighted with a keyword that you want to rank. And if possible, add a H2 or a H3 tag on the link.*

SEO for WordPress Blogs
Rank #1 on Google in any Niche or Keywords Guaranteed
Search Engine Optimization White Hat Practice to Rank High on Google and Other
Major Search Engines (Boost your SERP)

But do not overdue with inner links, focus on the content first and do inner linking after getting your websites and blogs ranked.

Offsite SEO

You need backlinks and in the past people used to do link farm techniques means creating lots of low quality Web2.0 sites linking to your main site. This type of backlinking is seen as Black Hat SEO by Google and other major search engines. Therefore, you must avoid them.

White Hat backlinking is what we will focus on. And its starts with social media sites such as Facebook, Twitter, YouTube, Instagram, Pinterest and Quora. You want to have backlinks from these sources. Ideally you want to have backlinks for Amazon, BBC and other highly ranked websites. However, placing a link in them is very hard. If you focus solely on the social media backlinks you should be alright to rank high on Google.

Quality over quantity. Google wants quality content not poorly writing content and vast quality. If you have quality content you will reach and ranked #1 on Google and other major search engines.

This is the safest way to do White Hat SEO. It takes time

SEO for WordPress Blogs
Rank #1 on Google in any Niche or Keywords Guaranteed
Search Engine Optimization White Hat Practice to Rank High on Google and Other
Major Search Engines (Boost your SERP)

at least 6 months to get noticeable results but it is guaranteed to work. The offsite on SEO should be done on daily based and making sure that you are not seen as a spammer. The quality content that you will create must get a buzz on the social media.

With time you will see naturally a social media viral result from your quality content and an uplift of your web rankings. This is done very smoothly with time.

Focus on quality content and you will rule the web and the search engines.

Social Media Marketing

Figure 3 - Social Media

SEO for WordPress Blogs
Rank #1 on Google in any Niche or Keywords Guaranteed
Search Engine Optimization White Hat Practice to Rank High on Google and Other
Major Search Engines (Boost your SERP)

To get social media content viral you must use #hashtags wisely and this applies to all social media platforms (Facebook, Twitter, YouTube, Pinterest, Instagram, etc).

Make sure that your social media content is quality not useless junk like the majority of the web. Use page titles and meta data carefully with useful content and highlight the keywords with hashtags. But do it in a way that is humanly readable and put 2 backlinks pointing to your WordPress blog. This is done naturally if you do it the right way. 100% White Hat method that works.

Make sure that your content that you deliver on the social media is quality and the meta data with hashtags must also match the same criteria. Make sure that it is humanly readable and has at least 800 words. With many hashtags and 2 links pointing to your blog. The number of hashtags makes a huge difference in terms of how many people will read or watch your social media content. The way to do viral marketing is to make sure that you highlight each and every single keyword with a hashtag inside your content or meta data.

2 links pointing to your blog will give link juice and over time you should ranked #1 on search engines and have lots of organic and social web traffic.

Answer quality answers on Quora pointing a link to your

SEO for WordPress Blogs
Rank #1 on Google in any Niche or Keywords Guaranteed
Search Engine Optimization White Hat Practice to Rank High on Google and Other
Major Search Engines (Boost your SERP)

blog for more details, this platform is widely use to get quality backlinks and traffic. I personally make lots of affiliate sales by answering Quora questions. My web traffic also increased and my blogs got enough link juice from this quality platform.

Yahoo Answer is another place, however there is no link juice. There are many quality platforms that you can use to get link juice. BBC, Amazon and eBay are just some of them.

Avoid Web2.0 and Squidoo Lenses. These sorts of platforms are no longer in use for White Hat SEO. If you have lots of backlinks from these sources this may be the reason why you got penalised by Google. The good news is that you can reverse this by following the right Google guidelines. Remove all the backlink juice and give some time to see results. Focus on social media and onsite SEO.

SEO for WordPress Blogs
Rank #1 on Google in any Niche or Keywords Guaranteed
Search Engine Optimization White Hat Practice to Rank High on Google and Other
Major Search Engines (Boost your SERP)

Ads and Affiliate Links

Figure 4 - Web Ads

If you are a webmaster the chances are likely that you have used affiliate links or advertisement links on your blog to get some sort of revenue. I have done this too and still do it. With the latest Google guidelines this also affects how search engines sees your website and how it ranks them.

A blog with little and poorly written quality posts with many affiliate and advertisements are seen as a link farm or Black Hat. Therefore, focus on quality content, at least posts of 800 words or more and the make sure that the advertisements or affiliate links come after the

SEO for WordPress Blogs
Rank #1 on Google in any Niche or Keywords Guaranteed
Search Engine Optimization White Hat Practice to Rank High on Google and Other
Major Search Engines (Boost your SERP)

fold of the website or blog. Any advertisement above the fold will be penalised by Google and other major search engines.

WordPress Themes

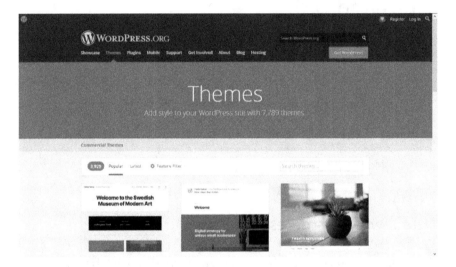

Figure 5 - https://wordpress.org/themes/

Believe it or not but certain themes will penalize your rankings. Therefore, making sure that you use WordPress themes that put the content above the fold. Quality content above the fold. A theme that has big letters or advertisements above the fold will be penalised. Likewise, a theme that makes sure that the content is delivered above the fold will increase the chances of the website or blog to rank quicker and

SEO for WordPress Blogs
Rank #1 on Google in any Niche or Keywords Guaranteed
Search Engine Optimization White Hat Practice to Rank High on Google and Other
Major Search Engines (Boost your SERP)

higher on the major search engines.

Links and URL

A little bit about onsite SEO and links or URLs. Make sure that your WordPress is setup as such that the URL links goes as follows: (the permalinks should be setup as follows):

Post name
http://www.wordpress.com/sample-post/

Having the www. In the beginning and a SEO friendly URL will ensure that your onsite SEO is working. For a human a website without the www. Will point to the site with www. As per backlinks if you have 2 types of links pointing to the same page one with www. And other without the www. The link juice will get divided which is not good for SEO purpose.

This is why you want to make sure that your domain structure or permalinks structure contains the www. In the beginning and has a post name afterwards. Avoid

SEO for WordPress Blogs
Rank #1 on Google in any Niche or Keywords Guaranteed
Search Engine Optimization White Hat Practice to Rank High on Google and Other
Major Search Engines (Boost your SERP)

having a category posts in the permalinks. However, if you want to focus on a keyword that uses your category has a permalink you can use that one for more friendlier SEO link structure. I personally avoid using categories. But it is totally after you.

Another thing to make sure is to avoid tags on your WordPress blog. If you want to use tags please make sure that they are not included on your sitemap.xml file. You do not want to index tag pages. Indexing tag pages will cause a huge drop on rankings and the blog will be seen as a spam blog. I personally never use tags on my WordPress blogs. But if you want to use it, make sure that it does not get into the sitemap.xml file. You can do that from the Yoast WordPress plugin setup.

SEO for WordPress Blogs
Rank #1 on Google in any Niche or Keywords Guaranteed
Search Engine Optimization White Hat Practice to Rank High on Google and Other
Major Search Engines (Boost your SERP)

Google Analytics

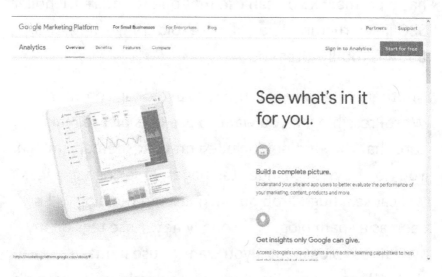

Figure 6 - https://marketingplatform.google.com/about/analytics/

In order to track your rankings and SEO progress you want to install Google Analytics to your blogs. The time that a user spends on your site will be a factor in how your WordPress blogs will be ranked. A higher bouncing rate will cause a drop on rankings. Therefore, you want to make sure that you deliver quality content on your site.

Google now ranks mobile friendly pages first and categorises how that entire site will be ranked. You want to make sure that your WordPress blog is mobile friendly. Use WordPress themes wisely, make sure that

SEO for WordPress Blogs
Rank #1 on Google in any Niche or Keywords Guaranteed
Search Engine Optimization White Hat Practice to Rank High on Google and Other
Major Search Engines (Boost your SERP)

the theme is SEO friendly. Meaning it is mobile friendly
and has content above the fold.

Sitemap and Webmaster Tools

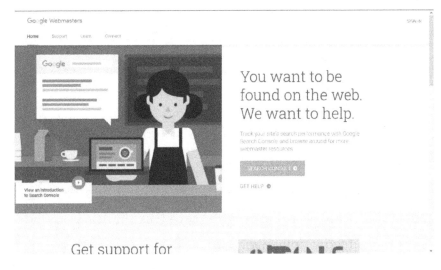

Figure 7 - https://www.google.com/webmasters/

SEO for WordPress Blogs
Rank #1 on Google in any Niche or Keywords Guaranteed
Search Engine Optimization White Hat Practice to Rank High on Google and Other
Major Search Engines (Boost your SERP)

Figure 8 - https://www.bing.com/toolbox/webmaster

In order to index your WordPress blog, you need to submit your xml sitemap to the search engines. The Yoast SEO Plugin will auto generate this file for you. Simple go to the following URL

http://www.yoursitedomain.com/sitemap.xml

in order to submit this file that contains all the links of your blog you need to go to:

https://www.google.com/webmasters/ and
https://www.bing.com/toolbox/webmaster

There you will be able to submit your site sitemap file. It takes a few days or week to your pages to get index by the major search engines. A quicker way to get index is to share your links in social media straight after

SEO for WordPress Blogs
Rank #1 on Google in any Niche or Keywords Guaranteed
Search Engine Optimization White Hat Practice to Rank High on Google and Other
Major Search Engines (Boost your SERP)

publishing the post. The sitemap file will auto generate those links; therefore, you do not need to submit this file every time.

You can also track the progress how the pages are ranked on the search engines. You can check how many pages are indexed, how much traffic are you getting for the search engines and how many people have seen your ranked pages on the search engine.

Keywords

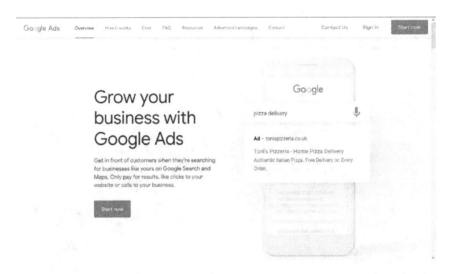

Figure 9 - https://ads.google.com/intl/en_uk/home/

A good way to find quality keywords is to use the Google Keyword Tool at

https://ads.google.com/intl/en_uk/home/tools/keywo

SEO for WordPress Blogs
Rank #1 on Google in any Niche or Keywords Guaranteed
Search Engine Optimization White Hat Practice to Rank High on Google and Other
Major Search Engines (Boost your SERP)

rd-planner/

You need to have a Google Ads account to use the tool. This tool will help you to find which keywords that popular and easy to rank. You also need to make sure that you use these keywords on the page title, meta description and image alt tags. Your blogpost also should mention these keywords in a human readable form. Also highlighting these keywords with H2, H3 or H4 tags will ensure that your onsite SEO is at a good standard. You will be able to rank with quality content. SEO on onsite just has to be humanly readable.

Comments and Spam Links

Figure 10 - Facebook comments

SEO for WordPress Blogs
Rank #1 on Google in any Niche or Keywords Guaranteed
Search Engine Optimization White Hat Practice to Rank High on Google and Other
Major Search Engines (Boost your SERP)

As a webmaster you must keep your blogposts comments updated, people will spam your blogs with useless comments. Therefore, make sure that you only approve certain type of comment. Also keep wary of hidden text. Black Hat techniques will not work and many people may still find your blog as a way to perform Black Hat techniques. This will harm your blog and your website. As a webmaster you must ensure that the content on your site matches the quality of Google and other major search engines. Following the guidelines will ensure that you rank #1 on major search engines.

You as a webmaster must make sure that you also do not get into trouble by doing any sort of Black Hat technique. Avoid spamming with useless content on other people blogs. In the past many used to hide content on the page, highlighting certain keywords this is another form of Black Hat technique. Avoid this from of practice. If you however possessed a website with this sort of content, I highly recommend you to revoke all Back Hat and resubmit your sitemap and wait a few months to get positive results.

Focus of pure 100% White Hat SEO and you should reach the number #1 spot on major search engines in any keyword or niche. It is true that Google and other major search engines will allow certain degree of Grey Hat SEO

SEO for WordPress Blogs
Rank #1 on Google in any Niche or Keywords Guaranteed
Search Engine Optimization White Hat Practice to Rank High on Google and Other
Major Search Engines (Boost your SERP)

on newly built websites, however the best practice is to do 100% White Hat SEO. Doing Grey Hat SEO will eventually damage your site authority and thus the rankings.

What I meant to say is that newly built WordPress blogs has a higher tolerance level of Grey Hat SEO compared to aged domains. If you have an aged domain and got penalised with rankings, my advice is to revoke all the Grey Hat stuff and focus of White Hat methods and resubmit your sitemap to Google and other major search engines. You will need to wait few weeks of months to notice positive results. But eventually, if done within the guidelines there is no reason why you should not reach #1 spot on Google and other major search engines.

SEO for WordPress Blogs
Rank #1 on Google in any Niche or Keywords Guaranteed
Search Engine Optimization White Hat Practice to Rank High on Google and Other
Major Search Engines (Boost your SERP)

Exact Match Domain or EMD and SEO

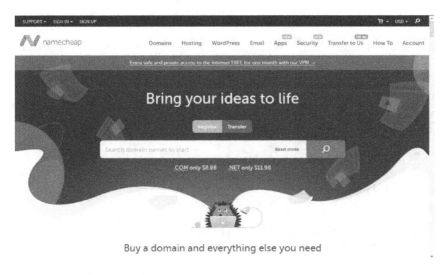

Figure 11 - https://www.namecheap.com/ - cheapest website to buy a domain name

After Panda, Penguin and Hummingbird Google updates.

SEO for WordPress Blogs
Rank #1 on Google in any Niche or Keywords Guaranteed
Search Engine Optimization White Hat Practice to Rank High on Google and Other
Major Search Engines (Boost your SERP)

Somewhere in there Google had updated their algorithm regarding EMD or Exact Domain Match. People in the past used to register domains with exact keywords in order to rank on Google and other major search engines.

This worked very well in the past but since the EMD algorithm update this practice become useless. This is however not a Black or Grey Hat technique. It is simply a way to rank well on search engines. In the past it works very well. Nowadays exact domain names and other branded domain names are ranked equally. Meaning the advantage of having a keyword rich domain has lost its value. This means any domain within the Google guidelines can rank very high on the major search engines.

Not finding a keyword rich domain will not damage or disvalue your website as per new Google algorithm updates. Just follow the guidelines, do 100% White Hat SEO and you will reach the top of the google search engine results or SERP.

Stand Out as a Brand Online

SEO for WordPress Blogs
Rank #1 on Google in any Niche or Keywords Guaranteed
Search Engine Optimization White Hat Practice to Rank High on Google and Other
Major Search Engines (Boost your SERP)

Figure 12 - https://www.facebook.com/smitchacha87

Furthermore, regarding White Hat SEO, you should focus to stand out as a brand online. This does not necessarily mean to have just a Facebook Fan Page, but also a WordPress blog that is seen as a brand online.

If you do a simple search of people who stand out in front of the crowd, such as: politicians, musicians, authors, actors, etc. You will notice that their picture and an excerpt of the tiny biography will appear in the search engines side bar.

This means they stand out in front of the crowd. They are a brand, and the process to do this is very simple. You are either a: Politian, musician, author, actor or something else.

SEO for WordPress Blogs
Rank #1 on Google in any Niche or Keywords Guaranteed
Search Engine Optimization White Hat Practice to Rank High on Google and Other
Major Search Engines (Boost your SERP)

Join politics, do your work or start producing music on Apple, or write a book on Amazon KDP. This way you will stand out in front of the crowd and build an online brand.

You will need to proclaim your status with the search engines as they will automatically add your name and your portfolio in the side bar. Just upload your pictures and you will be famous online.

This is my online success page: https://g.co/kgs/yVNxZs

Figure 13 - Smit Chacha Standing Out

I will teach you everything here, just keep following my blogposts on regular bases. Following is not enough you should at least do the effort in turning into to a practical tutorial.

SEO for WordPress Blogs
Rank #1 on Google in any Niche or Keywords Guaranteed
Search Engine Optimization White Hat Practice to Rank High on Google and Other
Major Search Engines (Boost your SERP)

Social Media (Facebook, Twitter, YouTube, Pinterest, etc.)

Since the launch of social media websites and platforms marketing become even more easy. Social media platforms such as: Facebook, Twitter, YouTube, Pinterest, Instagram, etc. has revolutionized the online world. These platforms are great to produce and distribute your content. Nowadays it is estimated that people aged 18-65 spend at least 2 hours on social media each day. Teenagers and young adults spend even more time on these platforms. Advertising which once only happened on television, radio and newspapers became more online. Nowadays companies spend more money on online advertising than on television.

It is important to have social media accounts to get popularity online. You do not need every single one of them. There are so many social media platforms. You just need a few of them and they are: Facebook, Twitter, Instagram, Pinterest, YouTube and that is it.

For a blogger you will not need YouTube for a Vlogger YouTube is essential. Anyways it is good to have a YouTube account but it is not necessary.

SEO for WordPress Blogs
Rank #1 on Google in any Niche or Keywords Guaranteed
Search Engine Optimization White Hat Practice to Rank High on Google and Other
Major Search Engines (Boost your SERP)

You can also create an online radio that will be broadcast live but I am not going to touch on that chapter. You can write and publish books or in other words transform your blogpost into a physical book that will be on sale in many online retailers. I will be touching on this in greater detail in later chapters.

Writing is fun and if you love writing you will succeed on the online world. Google and other major search engines love unique content and people also crave for unique written content. Just keep writing and sooner or later you will be popular online.

Social Media and #Hashtage

The best way to go viral on social media is to have #hastags all over you posts, but not the entire post. Social Media platforms such as Facebook, Twitters, Instagram, Pinterest and others use this common method of hashtags.

A good way to add hashtags is to a complete sentence and the keywords that stand out should be turned into a hashtag, below an example

"A good way to write a #CV or #Resume is to have a maximum of 1 page as many #employers will skip the second page. For more CV writing #tips and #techniques

SEO for WordPress Blogs
Rank #1 on Google in any Niche or Keywords Guaranteed
Search Engine Optimization White Hat Practice to Rank High on Google and Other
Major Search Engines (Boost your SERP)

go to LINK and read the following blogpost LINK. Best #employment and #interview getting tips."

As you can see, I have 2 links and my post is embedded with hashtags that are keywords that I want to highlight. These sort of hashtags posts will have better viewing and clicking rates. For Facebook just share on groups that way it is.

Brands and Keyword

To start an online business or a WordPress blog you need to stand out as a brand. Find a good quality domain names are short and keyword rich. Meaning something short with your niche keyword in there. These are hard to find as most are already registered. At GoDaddy and other domain registration websites you can do a simple search of your desired domain name and it will tell you if it is available to register, if not they will suggest your variations of the same keyword that are available in the present market.

The reason why you should have a keyword rich domain

SEO for WordPress Blogs
Rank #1 on Google in any Niche or Keywords Guaranteed
Search Engine Optimization White Hat Practice to Rank High on Google and Other
Major Search Engines (Boost your SERP)

is for pure SEO basics. We discussed this SEO in earlier chapters. For now all you need to know is that SEO (search engine optimization) is the mechanics of how internet search marketing works. The more you optimize your online business (the more SEO friendly) the better it will rank online.

Your brand must contain your target keywords for easy SEO. However, you can still rank your websites or blog with totally unique name.

Try to choose a short keyword brand as it is easy to remember. Something without hyphens if you can. Long tailed keywords are easy to rank, however there are fewer searches going on the web.

Nowadays you can register a 2.0 domain extension and these are very good and clever way to rank high on the search engines, specially for local or mobile.

My advice is to spend enough time in finding the right domain name for your blog. Something short and easy to remember.

Again, you can also use the Google Keyword Search tool mentioned in the earlier chapters to find the right domain name. Finding what exactly people are searching about. With the 2.0 domain extensions, nowadays the

SEO for WordPress Blogs
Rank #1 on Google in any Niche or Keywords Guaranteed
Search Engine Optimization White Hat Practice to Rank High on Google and Other
Major Search Engines (Boost your SERP)

range to register the right domain has become a lot easier.

Install SEO Yoast WordPress plugin the start a WordPress blog.

Have a good 53 characters long page or post title and use your meta description with at least 3 to 4 keywords that you want to rank on the search engines.

You should also have an email subscribers form on your blog. A way to direct market your audience. This is not for SEO per say but for getting a ton of web traffic.

Having an email subscribers list means you can engage your audience directly and send them weekly or monthly newsletters and updates of your latest posts.

This is a very common practice for many webmasters, we will touch on this in detail in later chapters. But for now I just want you to know that despite SEO there are other things you can do to get targeted web traffic.

SEO for WordPress Blogs
Rank #1 on Google in any Niche or Keywords Guaranteed
Search Engine Optimization White Hat Practice to Rank High on Google and Other
Major Search Engines (Boost your SERP)

Writing Blogposts on Your WordPress Blog

Once you have chosen your preferred web host install WordPress with your credentials such as page title, username, email and click on install. You will receive an email with your password which you can change it to whatever you want under the WordPress Dashboard (on user tab).

Change your password and it is recommended that you also change the permalinks to blogpost. It's a good SEO standard to rank pages under this sort of permalinks.

There are many SEO plugins that you can install the most popular is SEO Yoast, easy to install and to create xml sitemaps, which you can submit on Google Webmaster and Bing Webmaster tools. You need an xml sitemap in order to index your pages, posts and websites to Search Engines.

In WordPress there are many free and paid themes that you can choose and activate. Choose a theme and start blogging and writing blogpost. If you have installed SEO Yoast you can set the page title and meta description in order to better rank on Search Engines.

SEO for WordPress Blogs
Rank #1 on Google in any Niche or Keywords Guaranteed
Search Engine Optimization White Hat Practice to Rank High on Google and Other
Major Search Engines (Boost your SERP)

You can add categories, menus and even widgets under those tabs. You can even customize the CSS in most themes, including the free ones. WordPress is very easy to use and fun to publish articles, blogposts, etc.

Tip: There is a Twenty Twelve WordPress Theme which is fully customizable using CSS and there are thousands of online resources in how to create your very own WordPress theme from this one as a child theme.

You want to deliver quality content to your readers, quality over quantity. Google and other major search engines are now very cleaver in finding what is quality and what is pure junk and mass quantity.

In order to rank #1 on Google and other search engines you must write quality content. Focus on your keywords in a way that is humanly readable. Highlight your chosen keywords with headers (H1, H2, H3 or H4).

Your hyperlinks should also be highlighted with a header tag. You can customize your headers in external style sheet or should I say a custom style sheet. For this you must know how HTML/CSS.

If you do now know web design or web programing, I suggest you spend some time in searching for the right WordPress theme. There are thousands of popular free

SEO for WordPress Blogs
Rank #1 on Google in any Niche or Keywords Guaranteed
Search Engine Optimization White Hat Practice to Rank High on Google and Other
Major Search Engines (Boost your SERP)

themes that Google and other major search engines love and rank them very high on the search results or SERP.

Email Marketing and Email Subscribers List

As I said earlier a good way to direct market your audience is to have an email subscribers form in your blog. This is a very common practice and successful webmasters profit a lot in this form of direct marketing.

It does not matter if you have a blog or a YouTube Channel, you must have an email subscribers list to make sure that your targeted audience gets the message you want to share.

Therefore, to market your products and to make user engagements with your WordPress blog have an email subscribers list. Where users can input their name and email address and you can send me daily, weekly, monthly or periodically updates via email.

This way you will have a list of subscribers which you can later on send them newsletters or even physical products based on your blog niche. You will be able to do affiliate marketing via email which you can blast to

SEO for WordPress Blogs
Rank #1 on Google in any Niche or Keywords Guaranteed
Search Engine Optimization White Hat Practice to Rank High on Google and Other
Major Search Engines (Boost your SERP)

your followed subscribers and earn hundreds if not thousands of dollars' worth of commissions. This is a common and successfully marketing practice done worldwide with many branded blogs and brands.

You can even launch you own product and market it via email and get people know better your own products. The best way to do email marketing is to make sure that your emails do not go to spam folders. To do that you must let the user have the decency to double opt in to your list.

Meaning they should receive 2 emails once stating that they should confirm your email address and mark as non-spam (safe list). This way you will make sure that they always read your emails and they are not sent to their spam folder and ignored.

There are many email marketing services you can use, such as Aweber.com they charge a monthly fee and gets a bit expensive on the long run.

My advice is to use Sendy by Amazon, you can send 1000 emails for just $1 and there is a limit of 50000 emails per day. Which you can ask to increase later on once you have stablished a huge email list. Just search Sendy Amazon email marketing and you should find the web address or go to https://sendy.co/

SEO for WordPress Blogs
Rank #1 on Google in any Niche or Keywords Guaranteed
Search Engine Optimization White Hat Practice to Rank High on Google and Other
Major Search Engines (Boost your SERP)

Figure 14 - https://sendy.co/

It is very easy to install on your web server, just follow
the guidelines and they have an excellent customer
service and a forum where you can ask for help. It cost
around $50 and it is a one-time investment. Not a
monthly service charge like Aweber and other email
marketing services out there.

SEO for WordPress Blogs
Rank #1 on Google in any Niche or Keywords Guaranteed
Search Engine Optimization White Hat Practice to Rank High on Google and Other
Major Search Engines (Boost your SERP)

Affiliate Marketing

Figure 15 - Affiliate Marketing

If you are a webmaster you have been contact with this
form of marketing called affiliate marketing. If not,
affiliate marketing simply means to promote other
people products (physical or digital) and get a

SEO for WordPress Blogs
Rank #1 on Google in any Niche or Keywords Guaranteed
Search Engine Optimization White Hat Practice to Rank High on Google and Other
Major Search Engines (Boost your SERP)

commission in return.

It is a way to get some sort of income from your WordPress blogs. You can add banners and links on your blogpost that will redirect the user to your affiliate merchant page and if that click gets a sale you get a commission.

You get a percentage of the product price as a commission and you will be paid directly by the company or affiliate network where you are registered.

There are many affiliate networks out there below are some examples:

- Clickbank.com
- Cj.com (commission junction)
- Markethealth.com
- Sellhepalth.com
- Amazon affiliate program (amazon associates)
- And many more, just do a search on google "affiliate programs" or "affiliate networks" etc

With Amazon affiliate program you can earn up to 4% of each products cost as a form of a commission. The cookie that tracks your affiliate id last only 24 hours, meaning they can purchase any product in 24 hours after being sent to amazon by your affiliate link and you still get a commission. People earn hundreds if not

SEO for WordPress Blogs
Rank #1 on Google in any Niche or Keywords Guaranteed
Search Engine Optimization White Hat Practice to Rank High on Google and Other
Major Search Engines (Boost your SERP)

thousands of dollars a month with affiliate products.

And a nice thing about Amazon affiliate links is that they tend to blend very easily and looks good. Just go to https://affiliate-program.amazon.com/ and open an account and follow the guidelines and you should be good to go.

You can track your affiliate links with a unique affiliate id it is highly recommended that you use at least one id per blog, so you can track and tweak your affiliate links and check your progress.

Amazon pays you every 60 days, meaning for the first payment you will need to wait 60 days and then onwards you should be paid regularly. Just read their terms and conditions, follow their easy to read guidelines and you should be ready to go.

Adsense and Google Ads

Another good way to monetarise your blogs is with Adsense ads by Google. Just go to https://www.google.com/adsense/start/ and open an Adsense account and start putting Google ads on your blogpost. Your ads will be related to your blogpost and will blend entirely with your blogpost.

SEO for WordPress Blogs
Rank #1 on Google in any Niche or Keywords Guaranteed
Search Engine Optimization White Hat Practice to Rank High on Google and Other
Major Search Engines (Boost your SERP)

You earn a commission per click, meaning every time a user clicks on your Google ads you will get a commission, this can range from $0.01 to $10 solely based on how expensive the ad is. People can make a living based solely on Google Adsense advertisements. They need to write quality and unique content on daily bases to archive that goal.

Again, read a follow all Google Adsense guidelines and terms and you should be ready to go.

Google Adsense is a popular way to find paid advertisers on your blog. Many webmasters make a living solely on Google Adsense ads. However, for a SEO stand point you must focus on quality content rather that advertisements.

Put your quality content first, above the fold and target your audience with quality content. A page with full of ads and little content will be seen as a spam to Google and other search engines.

This will get you penalized on Google search results. It could even de-index your pages altogether. Follow the Google guidelines and do pure 100% White Hat SEO and you should be good to go.

SEO for WordPress Blogs
Rank #1 on Google in any Niche or Keywords Guaranteed
Search Engine Optimization White Hat Practice to Rank High on Google and Other
Major Search Engines (Boost your SERP)

From Blogpost to a Paperback Book

Figure 16 - https://www.lulu.com/

Did you know you can also transform your blogpost into physical book where you can royalties based on sales. It is a common practice for many bloggers. They start an online blog and write hundreds of posts and once they are written everything that there is in their niche, they select certain blogposts and transform it into a paperback book.

You can do that on Amazon KDP or via a publisher such as lulu.com

SEO for WordPress Blogs
Rank #1 on Google in any Niche or Keywords Guaranteed
Search Engine Optimization White Hat Practice to Rank High on Google and Other
Major Search Engines (Boost your SERP)

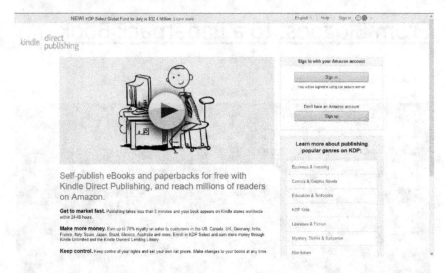

Figure 17 - https://kdp.amazon.com/en_US/

Again, follow the guidelines and you should be ok to go and become an author from a blogger. You will have a Google profile page on the right side with you picture and your books. Whenever people search for your name. Here is an example of mine: search "Smit Chacha" without quotes and you should see my profile picture on Google.

So that it is it, I hope you enjoyed reading this book and for more of my books search on Google, Amazon and other book stores.

SEO for WordPress Blogs
Rank #1 on Google in any Niche or Keywords Guaranteed
Search Engine Optimization White Hat Practice to Rank High on Google and Other
Major Search Engines (Boost your SERP)

Sell Your Website on Flippa.com

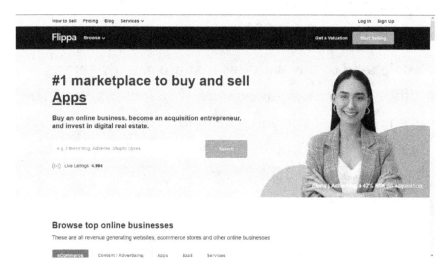

Figure 18 - https://flippa.com/

Finally, I want to end the chapter and the book with a tip in how to sell your website or blog on flippa.com

Flippa.com is an online platform where people can buy and sell stablished websites and it cost around $49 to insert an adverted. Flippa also charges 10% commission

SEO for WordPress Blogs
Rank #1 on Google in any Niche or Keywords Guaranteed
Search Engine Optimization White Hat Practice to Rank High on Google and Other
Major Search Engines (Boost your SERP)

per sale for websites sold under $50k

I have sold multiple blogs and websites on Flippa on an average of $6000 per WordPress blog. u blogs where sold simply because they were getting tons of web organic traffic and revenue.

For example, if your blog gets around 1500 visitors a month and you earn around $200 a month with Clickbank, Amazon or AdSense you can estimate to your website to be sold at $6000.

People tend to buy websites that are already getting traffic and revenue. An average of 36 months' worth of revenue is what you should aim for. There are sites sold for over 1 million dollars but those websites traffic and revenue is around $50k a month.

ABOUT THE AUTHOR

Smit Chacha is an author, writer, web developer, affiliate marker and forex trader who has published several books. He is an online blogger and has published over 400 articles on EzineArticles.com, under his and other pet names. For the past 10 years he has developed and managed several blogs and e-commerce websites.

www.ingramcontent.com/pod-product-compliance
Lightning Source LLC
LaVergne TN
LVHW051622050326
832903LV00033B/4625